D0934327

FLIGHT PATTERNS

10/14/89

for Leda

with warmest best wishes
for life and love,

Lisa

FLight

PATTERNS

Lisa Ress (signature)

LISA RESS

UNIVERSITY PRESS OF VIRGINIA
CHARLOTTESVILLE

For my mother,
my father,
my grandparents who got away,
my grandparents who didn't get away,
and all of us who disappear.

THE UNIVERSITY PRESS OF VIRGINIA
Copyright © 1985 by the Rector and Visitors
of the University of Virginia

First published 1985

Library of Congress Cataloging in Publication Data

Ress, Lisa.
Flight Patterns.

I. Title.
PS3568.E73F54   1984   811'.54   84–19687
ISBN 0–8139–1053–6

Printed in the United States of America

The dedication for Lisa Ress's *Flight Patterns* reads: "For my mother, my father, my grandparents who got away, my grandparents who didn't get away, and all of us who disappear." The book's first section relates directly to that dedication, and is powerful and moving stuff. The vividness of the family history and memories might easily have led to that poetry which holds tenaciously to past tragedies and wrongs as the only legitimate source of work. Instead, it is deepened and melded into both the sense of all human vulnerability, and an extraordinary appreciation of the accidents of joy. Ress has made a fine and unusual passage between the poetry that deals with the personal problems and actions of the poet and the poetry that struggles with the responsibility to represent its time.

The knowledge of power and cruelty are always there—in "the pound of the flicker hammering bark for a meal." She hears the drumming,

> nearly the sound my great-grandmother knew
> that summer in Poland when
> tending the geese at the edge of her village she heard
> the rip of hooves ridden hard toward her, striking into
>   the ground.

The permanent consciousness of the dead serves to feed the living. In a grim, but ultimately gentle poem, a woman who has revisited Auschwitz speaks:

> I learned
> to take nothing from the living,
> but the dead don't need

their bread ration,
don't need their thin clothes,
their broken
real leather shoes.
Take from the dead.

The taking, in various levels, eventually serves a sense of enrich-
ment, a depth of proportion, an acute sense of vitality; this lighted
both by the sense of abrupt joys and imminent disasters. The poetry
is extraordinarily alive.

So many bad poems have been written about the giant and ter-
rible events of the past half century; it requires temerity, and often
hubris, to take on the magnitude of such events. The first part of
Flight Patterns deals with them or their effects; but they are repre-
sented by a simplicity of detail, a grasp of proportion, which si-
multaneously gives them reality and ties them; to daily humanity.

Ress never strays into the abstract, the generalization. She has an
acute sense of the human's relation to the earth itself, and the
manifestations of its wildly varied life are precious to her, and
expressed with vividness and control. Emotional experiences live in
physical, almost tangible terms. A parting is also the house in
which it happened:

Failed house, skull house
from which all features
are eaten away, the furniture brief
statements of loss,
parted by outbursts of ash.
Hill house, the wasps
spitting their nests into every crack
and fault.

And in the same way, joy and growth are direct as physical manifestations:

> where I set out bulbs like prayers
> and each repaid me,
> licking my fingers with its dark
> or colored tongue,
> leaving its love in the grooves of my wrinkling
> hands become like wood
> or soil itself, like loam or bark,
> twiglike, efflorescent and branching.

At a moment when much poetry fears directness as the creeping cousin of superficiality, Ress is extraordinarily mature in her ability to convey levels, shadows, intimations, in language which is both lucid and active. The directness of her language carries with it nuances, consciousness of relationships, which show remarkable control. She has managed never to confuse abstractions with intellect, freedom of movement with formlessness. The poetry moves with confidence and originality in its firm direction. In this book, reader and poet meet in an admirable series of discoveries.

JOSEPHINE JACOBSEN

ACKNOWLEDGMENTS

The author and publisher wish to thank the following magazines and anthologies
for permission to reprint certain poems:

Artemis for "And Green Again," "Bench in the Garden," "Gum Trouble,"
"Targeted," and "Trip to the Junk Store with the Blue-eyed Man"

Audit for "Connection," "The Harbor," "Household Rules," "Igor, My Pnin,"
"Learning the Ropes," "Montrose Beach," "Synagogue," "U.S. Army
Holds Dance for Camp Survivors," and "Waving Her Farewell"

The Black Warrior Review for "Belvedere Palace and Favoritenstrasse"

Black Willow for "Round Trip"

Columbia for "Route 11 South towards Christiansburg" and "Traveling
through Pictures of China"

Green Revolution for "Here's the Contract"

Kalliope for "Bombings at Christmas," "Hostage," "She Calls Me," and "Songs
She Sings Are Songs Sung Her"

Kudzu for "Goose Girl" and "Graduate Record Exam"

The Madison Review for "The Opera Is Fully Restored"

The Mid-Atlantic Review for "Incest"

MSS for "War Movie over Iowa"

Outerbridge for "Feeding the Animals in Winter" and "Taking Down the Barn"

Prairie Schooner for "Late Spring Trip," "One of Everything, Two of Us," and
"Spaghetti Sauce, Good Red." Reprinted from *Prairie Schooner*, by permis-
sion of University of Nebraska Press. Copyright 1984 University of Ne-
braska Press.

Saturday's Women for "Grandmother's House: The Baba Yaga"

13th Moon for "Happy Birthday, Happy Birthday, Happy Birthday, Dear
Mom"

Ubu for "Family Album" and "Walter von der Vogelweide and I"

I wish to express my gratitude to the Virginia Center for the Creative Arts,
whose support enabled me to write the opening sequence of poems, to Valery
Nash, Natalie Sheffler, and Dara Wier, whose wisdom, acuity and devotion to
craft helped these poems into form, and to A. R. Ammons for his support and for
his light.

Human nature is like a great war, it makes you nervous. . . . And politics and geography and government and propaganda, well and what of it what of politics and geography and government and money and propaganda, do they make you nervous. Do they.

GERTRUDE STEIN

CONTENTS

1

TAKING IN THE AUGUSTINERSTRASSE.

VIENNA IV, 1958

Store glass reflects me imperfectly. It is busy with cake
set in landscapes of fruit tarts, éclairs
dreamed by a child fitted only for pleasure.

Black gates keep the sweet fruit from me.
Block after block, the buildings unite. I am disparate,
wavering from tree to tree under their high and radiant bloom.

Again it is fall without summer. Leaves clutch at the pavement,
yellow as Tante Lina's hands on the hospital sheet, my mother's last
childhood kin, shrunken beneath the tall Jesus commanding
        the wall.

These walls that line the street here make my shoulders ache with
        their permanence.
I can read what their pitted stutter spells: machine-gun fire,
written at the level of my neck in filaments of white and red
        seized from the living.

At my feet the Karlsplatz spreads like a cushion, the church
hilarious in pink and white and green. There is the gaiety
        of the tram,
the rhythmic pounding of the dead against the simple surface
        of the present.

WAVING HER FAREWELL. TRAIN STATION,

VIENNA XV, 1939

It is not a trip to the Prater or Augarten to play.
On the train seat, a basket,
two rolls, the last butter. Behind her
massed parents, the platform blurred with coats.
Years forward she will waken still telling over faces of the dead.
The count, not finished at nightfall, awaits.
No one will like her dark looks.
She has tasks.
Inside her cupped palms, the city, thousand years,
the wailing shades.
She wails back,
sucked forward to the tunnel, sent
with weeping children into immigration sheds at Dover.
Someone else's life, she thinks. How mine?
Wiping the dirt from the window, a circle for her eye
and everywhere the tunnel
howling at both mouths.

For Jessica Mann   4

THE HARBOR. TANGIER, 1940

The room that sheltered me at birth resides
in neural passageways among thick houses, white,
sea glare like paint on buttresses behind tough-fingered trees
from which the fruit peers, juice-soft, in rind.
It is the corner of a film frame moving from me as I sleep or sail.

Palms, named after hands, there hold their leaves out to me.
Flat-petaled roses fuse.
My mother leans against the windowsill, her elbows sharp,
she holds me up, turns me to see the ships
bombed ragged in the harbor.

CONNECTION. AUSCHWITZ, 1941

A woman whose joints are knobbed like receivers on phones
lies in her dirt on a wooden slab.

You can call to her. Remember.

She dreams of a sky filled with birds
perched on wires strung over fields near your town.

You can see them from your window, knobbing the line.

The woman turns on her arms,
every joint a bird, shouting down the line, saying your name.

U.S. ARMY HOLDS DANCE FOR CAMP SURVIVORS.

GERMANY, 1945

We recognize each other, neighbors before the war,
schoolmates until the schools shut against us.
Our families hid past the coalbins,
the children's mouths taped, our heads swollen with sound.
You kept on with your piano lessons,
the silence of the Czerny exercises eroding
the black- and white-painted board.
G.I.'s broke us from the camps.
Now we hold together, circling in time,
not the dead for whom we long, but like them.
Cracked open behind us, our cellars glow with our youth.

HOUSEHOLD RULES. FARWELL AVENUE,
CHICAGO, 1946

1

She turns onions into zeros on the cutting board,
lines up the sheets at the edges of the linen cupboard shelves.
At four o'clock exactly she is marching X's with her needle
uniformed in thread along the borders of a tablecloth.
She shows me how to get up the stairs, how to come down,
how to lie in bed so no one can find me.
The knock on the door of this house in this country
is that of the milkman.
But I know I must ask myself
what is milk, what is coal, what do they mean
saying "Good morning, Lisa," as I cross the street.

2

She papers the kitchen with pictures of bodies
tangled like insects in ditches.
This could be you, she tells me.
I am a child, I say. I am not
supposed to know this, knowing anyway
that soon, or yesterday, I will be one of them, I am.
Drink your milk, she says, but it is white
elixir that will make me live too long.
At school the kids push me flat against the chain link fence.
How shall I keep them from knowing
how far it is all right for them to go?

For Edith Heyer

SYNAGOGUE. ROGERS PARK, CHICAGO, 1947

Saturdays my grandpa leads me
through the mysteries of neighborhood.
We walk past sour-smelling bars, jewellike in neon,
past the Miller Hi-Life Girl, her skirt and perfect crescent,
past the tiny village carved by firemen,
set with mirror pools within a three-foot square.
He holds my hand.

We reach the place we always reach. We stand,
our heads tipped back, and stare at steps that rise
in tiers towards the dome that floats over us, mute, green,
smooth as my grandpa's head under clouds.
I wonder what the building is, what those
who climb the steps and enter through the wide bronze doors
might do in there. I wonder why we don't go in
but never ask. My grandpa's hand around my own
forgets me. Then we turn. His sigh,
like pigeons circling overhead, signs the day.

For Jacob Reiss

MONTROSE BEACH. CHICAGO, 1948

Anytime after a war any one is nervous. They think they
are excited but they are nervous.

GERTRUDE STEIN

Sundays we walk ten blocks to the lakeshore
with hampers of cakes and canasta cards, chicken
and folding chairs, card tables, my dad's
accordion in its cracked, red-lined case.
We fill up the streets, take over the hills.
They are ours, bright with our speech
that makes shapes that we know, sheltered
in gestures that are our home.
Even the children have appetite. Though there is always,
eyeing the trees,
one man, one woman, restlessly walking.

IGOR, MY PNIN. LAKEWOOD STREET,

CHICAGO, 1948

a fat glossy nose and innocent eyes . . . the physique of
old-fashioned intellectual Russia.

V. V. NABOKOV

He is on the phone again, asking to be allowed a visit.
He will bring anything, ice cream in three flavors,
    chocolates, tedium.
At the beach, that is him with his white sleeves rolled,
    his handkerchief
knotted to cover his baldness.
Playing with the phone cord, my grandmother twists her lips,
a noose pulled tight around his neck.
"Sto?" she cries, aping amazement. "Come over? No." She lies
carefully, so he will know how she despises him.

He brings me mints shaped like flowers, the sugar like
    gems or tears
sparkling in the light of our strangeness.
This new world, where cruelty was to have been left behind,
where his fat helpless hands should not have lived only to pack
a thin lunch for the office, to stroke in the evening
the velvet of curtains dividing two worlds,
each to one side of the darkening green.

LEARNING THE ROPES. CUSTER STREET,
EVANSTON, 1949

Showering, I see more than the single showerhead,
and test myself, how long I can go without breathing.
The icy road to school is my grandparents' way to the work camp.
I make it through.
The elevated is a cattle car that seals me in with strangers.
I study them. Who will be the first to crack?
Who will not look away when I have to go to the bathroom?

Sundays before our parents awake, my sister and I jump our
        wrecked ship,
hit the refrigerator for provisions to stock our beds.
We rescue each stuffed animal.
This time we will get away with our lives.

For Kathy, who always played shipwreck with me.   12

THE OPERA IS FULLY RESTORED. VIENNA I, 1957

Here and there a space in the building rows
lets the cold through.
Frost on the mortar, a shimmer like split glass.
In the parks are green niches.
No one will look for us anywhere.
There is so much food again.
We can eat quietly.
The sparrows are fat and the roofs only sheltering
hands or breasts spilling light.
The wall against which we became shadows
has been cleared away. The whole city
is being rebuilt.

AT YOUR TABLE. VIENNA V, 1957

You serve me on plates marked with my grandmother's monogram
left with you for safekeeping the day she ran.
You have untied the letters, let our name out, it is gone.
The language we share cracks in my mouth.
Your home, you say, your dishes now, your tongue
curled like the long arms of the boxwood that would not hold us.
Your parks, your stone musicians.
You with your passion for music, crying out as the bow
shudders over tight dried gut.

WALTER VON DER VOGELWEIDE AND I.

BOMBSITE, VIENNA X, 1958

Sifting through the hills of shoes and brick
I come across the pieces of his picture. He is singing,
seated in his bird-rich meadow on a rock,
his song his spine, his spine his house, his house
stone cellars stronger than the ones around me, Alps
his vertebrae. Robed in blue, his voice
builds chambers in the trees of throat-smoothed stone.
He nests. He shows me home as incantations catching shapes,
these, even, broken all around me, the remains of a world
sunk under nettles, their roots
binding them back into soil.

BELVEDERE PALACE AND FAVORITENSTRASSE.

VIENNA IV, 1958

I. IN THE HALL OF THE GIANTS WITH THE BLUE-EYED MAN.

I lean along the leg that swells against my cheek,
trace the toe as I might the mouth of a child.
I think the statue marble, he will teach me
it is stucco, hollow skin of stone.
The muscle fills my palm.
I scrutinize the blue-eyed man, his lesson
and his back to me, the whitened
jacket seam, broken at the shoulder.

II. IN THE PALACE GARDENS WITH THE MAN AND THE BATS

We reach a square of trees ranked clipped against the sky.
They will come, he tells me.
Taking out his handkerchief, throwing the white-wrapped rock.
The bats skim—fixed, fierce, angular,
with shining faces.
You see, he says. They play.

III. UP THE STAIRS AND INTO BED WITH THE BLUE-EYED MAN.

Climbing to his room my feet cannot tell
marble treads from bombed gaps filled with plaster.
Once inside I slide my hands along the white
and gilded stove tiles, press down stilled ivory keys.
Wrapped in sheets I follow cracks spread maplike overhead,
lean on his back, trace bony wings beneath his skin.

TRIP TO THE JUNK STORE WITH THE BLUE-EYED

MAN. VIENNA VII, 1958

At breakfast he tears the rolls into pieces,
spreads butter over sweet white bread.
Last night he leaped from the taxicab screaming,
resisted the vicious questions of lampposts,
grabbed strangers, told them he knew.

Now his hands shake only a little. My dear German
husband—and I—his loved Jewish wife. Six months since
    we married,
fixing ourselves in our exiles together, alive in this city that turned
on my family, in which I can walk now as much as I want to, where
nothing can ever be mine, as nothing German can ever be his.

When he was ten, he was sent to the country—Bavaria—for safety
from air raids, his boarding school there something like camp:
he was made to stand all night with his arms outstretched
    and weighted,
made to dress for meals in his own pissed-on sheets, forever
forbidden to speak in the small voice of his years.

He was thin when I met him, his cheekbones gone Polish
    with hunger,
his eyes still as miners' canaries taken down shafts.
Afternoons, in the old parts of town, I trail him.
Streets shift like dunes, restaurants rise like mirages, offer us
meals under porticos, leave us still empty, withdraw.

His face in the clear yellow light shows the dark of a dead eye-
tooth, the surface of his water eye impenetrable.
Straining, he sifts through junked objects like a child
wild to see life at the shore, each glittering sway of the tide
bringing relics he grasps at with trembling hands.

Forever beyond him the shimmering calm of his childhood
      brick house,
thatched roofs of the village, sunk as if lost under fathoms of sea.

For H.-J. W.   18

NEW WINE. VIENNA   XIX, 1959

My feet are the travelers, walking
transparent, like water
held in a glass. Through him
I made myself a body. And left him.
Now there is drifting through lamplight, a view
of my feet against cobblestones set like apples into the street.

Around me the music of zithers and fiddles forms eddies.
Past the wooden gate, people wait, not precisely for me.
Grapes in the passageway curl into crowns, they touch me,
curious, and trees against walls,
flattened like spies in old movies, look both ways.

I pass them, follow
the warmth of the stucco to tables and benches and chairs
set where the grass looks heavy and the dwarf trees stoop with fruit.
Sit down.
Here where my grandfather's sister and brothers
raised their glasses, staring through pears.

Light comes and goes, a gift, like the pictures they left me,
handfuls of rescued time. Moon flares in the arbor,
makes grapes white, candle fire
ripens the peaches and plums, turns faces to glowing fruit.
Guests, their hands sunk in silver and in yellow gold, splash light,
the taste of new wine a chord like wonder in everyone's mouth.

Dr. Bronowski stands in the marshes.
He has come back to Poland and squats in hard shoes,
scooping silt and pouring it hand to hand.
Here, says Dr. Bronowski, his glances
concentrating light,
are the ashes of four million people.
We watch the thin mud of our parents
slip through his hands.

He speaks to us wading. The wetness
climbs in his shoes. At the viscid center
the sky has become his eyes, the pond skin
folds itself against him, hugging his flesh.

For Sali and Frigyes Heyer

Some pages have eyes, some mouths. They desire.
Put a platter on. I want to dance at the Stadtpark Café.
They have papers to complete. Tax records haunt them.
Their secretaries, still on leave, were never notified when to return.
Each page has an aura of surprise.
I was just putting dinner on the table. Here is the book
I promised Max. Sidi has not spoken to her father.

They stare at me, move their lips.
Alive or dead, they ask,
their worried, torn-up faces stuck to the page.
I try to help. I call up music,
wide brass notes that tear them free.
We put our arms back, and our faces, lace our flesh.
We are one body, whole.
The city walls keep time, they spin with us,
one clamorous gold mote, dancing away.

Sitting on wide woooden steps that already seem old,
worn by weather and by light,
we watch the geese lurch on their orange feet, pull clover,
the day wrapping us. We're safe,
the geese at our feet calm with their legs stretched
lean their necks toward us,
sliding on currents of bird life, the turn
of mate to nest, rise of the newly hatched into sky or grass.

Here is our house in the fields. No neighbors.
Only low insect voices, no blood
on this peace. Today
no one will come here with weapons,
though on the edge
of a slow brown river
purple with weeds
there are scattered clay pots,
fires upset, soft bones and wet bellies.
The skin of the world widens until we can touch
the dark bank, trip in deep tracks bare running feet have made
getting away. It is the quiet that comes after sudden noise.

The pound of the flicker hammering bark for a meal
of soft grubs brings me back to the ache
in my leg pressed tight to the stair,
back to the tangle of boards thrown over the grass,
to the taint of kerosene spilled
when the lamp broke yesterday.

I hear the drumming, nearly the sound my great-
     grandmother knew
that summer in Poland when
tending the geese at the edge of her village she heard
the rip of hooves ridden hard toward her, striking into the ground.

You rub your knuckles on the walls
through which the fields beckon like bodies.
You want to get out
but the building has you in its dreams
and will not wake up.

The upward cry of a sycamore
made of raw patches
hurts your eyes. You draw it,
shape of a tune stopped in the throat.

Birds circle.

You look at spiked pits dug in jungles, threats
chalked on sidewalks, your son's
plastic soldiers underfoot on the stair.
A game, he tells you.
Bombs in the letters, first stone to star a skull.

Your fingers run on, tying you in with a bloody string.

BOMBINGS AT CHRISTMAS

Some days there is only pain and the sky
calm and mean as your father
who leans
over your hands stretched on the keyboard saying

wrong   wrong   wrong
the note is flawed the note you are
yours the flaw you

and of course the sky is large
drops fire sends wind in to stir it
awards you a season
trims you with tinsel tips you
out with the trees shedding needles
under its perfectly trained eye

On our way to the ball, black tie,
darkened car, and our best set of guns,
we meet another fast automobile.
But it is our party. We want to get there.
We want our hall full of faces, our photos
blown up to advantage, stroking the walls.

Every bush in the world has been marched to the roadside
with orders to cheer us in passing. They stare,
they are thin, and how fast we lose track; at our speed
who is to say where the road is?

Woods break the car wide. Our necks snap back.
This hungry wind chewing the skin from our cheeks
is our last. The air shakes us dry and the dust that we are
flies on through the doorways and empties the room.

WAR MOVIE OVER IOWA

Borne among separated lights, the stars'
cool blue, yellow-spattered plains, red jets
beating time, I clutch at the curl and roar
of long-extinct wild animals caught between the plastic
covers of the magazine that rides my lap.
In it I read that life is motion: at five hundred
miles per hour, think how I am living, looking
blindly over Ames and Denison.

On my right the movie screen
shows colored shapes, transparent apparitions, nearly
men, and moving warily.
Round as an animals's eye, the window
next to me endures what's printed there:
combatants, edgy, and in packs,
crossing the heavens with their guns unslung.

It should be dark, here and below, no flame
but the buffalo running firm
across webbed miles of roots, a darkness
cool on our bare arms raised
to call them to us.

The window glass floats streetlights through steel-toed
soldiers' shoes. No woods below.
Only the sky, and we are in it,
specks in the crystal leg of a beast
at rest in planetary depths.

I can stay in
as long as I like, the world
makes a pleasant
shape on the wall,
or I can sit looking out
at the snow. It fell
as I slept.

Spread out here beside me
a bank of white letters—Dear
Mr. Rudenko, Procurer General,
Moscow: Please note, Mr. Zhikarev,
now in the Psychiatric
Hospital, Chernyakhovsk, cannot
get out. Let him go. Most
honored Señores Pinochet, Galtieri:
Some thousands have vanished.
The waste spaces of towns fill with
fresh bodies. Please spare these,
your people.

Last night on TV
a woman named Kitty revisited
Auschwitz where she'd been
a girl. She said to her son:
to survive these deep winters
in Poland I learned
to take nothing from the living,
but the dead don't need

their bread ration,
don't need their thin clothes,
their broken
real leather shoes.
Take from the dead.

Crystal by crystal
ice covers the window
mimicking jungles
of ferns. In my dream
I felt life as a loosening
handshake, the impact of bodies
striking the ground.

I can
stay in
as long
as I like,
my desk under
snow. In my dream or
outside it,
clearing
pieces
of paper
away.
My eyes
fixed on my wall maps,
not on the hands wanting
water, reaching from
block 25, blood
the shape of all continents drying
on cellblock walls,
not on my joy:

It is not
my body splitting on stones.

This morning
nothing but ice on the window,
against it the sweet
curve of frost ferns,
against them,
my face.

I like to stay in.

GUM TROUBLE

The dentist probing pockets
of dead flesh between my teeth,
he knows the story:
the resounding tooth athwart
receding bone,
flesh fallen back from fine white fangs,
themselves a monument, renowned
examples of our building art,
but Mies and Corbusier, not
Gaudi, only blank walls rising
toward the function for which they're designed
and falling short because of rot in the foundation.

2

Is real, I think, because my kinfolk eat it.
Flecks of garlic rolling up,
dark basil stretching leaves into the boil.
Is real. But that
which makes the sauce, cuts onions square and small
is hard to come upon. It flickers, hides in slicing, lies.
Better to look at birds on the branch,
knowing nothing of birds on the branch.
And at the butcher's asking for a pound of meat,
the spread of crosscut fibers brightly red
and showing straight through my reflection in the case.
My face, lumpy, lost to me.
Easier to stare at you, the birds, the meat.
Better the sauce, its glow, and the eating.

GRANDMOTHER'S HOUSE: THE BABA YAGA

Yellow claws start from the pot,
blue chicken thighs are rigid on the plate.
She is sucking soup and chewing carefully.
Carp eyes in gelatin, glazed scales.
From the glassfront cabinet, my grandpa,
soft and hungry, stares.

I am six, I am eight, I am ten.
I am her juicy dove, her little eel and pigeon pie.

Inside the bed's white throat, my legs
lie stiff against the sheet.
All night she is brushing out her hair, stretching it.
Brushing out her hair, brushing mine,
winding the hanks on narrow spools.

Your eye at me, a bite
for your brain, laid out,
an experiment.
I was the baby you taught to swim,
throwing me into the freezer-sharp gel
of your fresh and icy brain cells.

A shock.
I went under and oh
the currents that flowed there
in your north sea.
The tops of the icebergs looked pure.
The bottoms were dirty with undersea life.
Your mind
a swarm of night-sucking insects
feeding on chill.
It was so still there.

I swam for life and crawled
much later through your bitter blue eye.

HAPPY BIRTHDAY HAPPY BIRTHDAY HAPPY
BIRTHDAY DEAR MOM

The teeny hectic boppin'
queen of my childhood days
swashing down the street in her
platform shoes, hips
raising steam
in the slow air,

her red-tipped hand erased me one
thousand times, she
put me back together each time
some part missing, each time
more tightly packed, more
loosely jointed, hollower,
more space given
her coal fires.

Mare of my dreams
she rides over
my birth furious, her
hooves strike sparks that make
today's light pale.

Waiting, the drift is her hair caught.
Tides swell but she floats slack.

Why doesn't she turn herself over, catch hold?

The sea is strong green, bites sharp.
Her arm has an empty hand at the end of it, fingers parted.

The twilight is like water on water.
The edge of the sea is near and the silence
is the sound of it falling.

SHE CALLS ME

My name,
called across the short wet grass. My name
among the columns and the lawns.
She calls me, she wants me, lovely. I turn.

There are gardens, hushed stones,
at the center a dial showing movement
that ends slowly, that lasts so long.
She calls me.

Two women on the quad embrace.
I turn again and send my fingers through my pockets.
There are toothpicks, little stones,
news of people in another town.

Without a mouth, what kisses? Rain
folds itself on me, an apron. Name.
The sound is loose, now, slipping down brick walls.
This perfect, empty, crafted space.

She calls me.
It is to pass through her red nails,
to sear staring at the white she bares,
bright as the place bone shows. Calling me.

And did she want me in to supper?
There was only her steel skirt, her wrists
springing against me, the rage of the stove
and how the kettle screamed each morning.

The sky is red and swells.
I am no secret.
The fire is full, is all
and how she touches me till I am burnt away.

ONE OF EVERYTHING, TWO OF US

Though you speak of finding a larger room later,
it is too late,
the wardrobe has taken my clothes.

You have the only chair,
sit hunched at the old L. C. Smith.
I move from window to door, circle the stove,
fall on the bed, cross my arms over my chest, picture the room
a coffin around me. There is your back,
dwindling as you race from me over the alphabet.

"Read a book," you insist,
knowing their pages refuse me.
"Let me out," I say.
"Women stay home," you lie, and I let you,
deeply annoyed and satisfied.
"Be good, oh be quiet."

Trying for calm you swear I can have
six Spanish blood oranges from market tomorrow
though they are still very dear.

For H.-J. W.

When we came to the Rhône
the bridge was chalky and broken,
the water glass green.
Everything else was white in my mouth,
tasted empty.
We couldn't cross.
I had been on the edge of that place
all along, straining to see to the farther
shore: flaking walls, chalk arches,
the citrus, the heat and the dust.

We ate fish at the Hôtel de la Poste.
Green beans obedient
lay in their dish, not soft, not hard,
a tender dark green.
I swallowed carefully,
not looking at you because you
weren't there, though your hand
opened and closed on the table.

I had to go back. All along I had known
I was holding bones in the guise
of my hands, my life
in the gaping between, that I could close
these spaces, I could
close them, and so
I went back to the shore.

IT SEEMS IT WASN'T YOU AT ALL

Grappling in the garden by the school
among the stiffened herbs, how firm our bodies there,
they sang like Chinese vases and our hips
rose from our thighs like wind lines bowing to the equinox.
We could have worn them anywhere
but we revealed them only secretly, white
in the darkness of parked cars,
light with a dry heaving lust ignorant of satiation.

Unbraided by the stroke of twenty years, my skin
hangs shimmering between your palms,
the mark of lovers, children, rooms unknown to you
imprinted as transparencies that shine through flesh.
I see the flesh falls from you too.
It had a shape we took for yours.
It seems it wasn't you at all. Time,
diligent Eskimo woman, has chewed us soft.

And you are angry now. You suck your rounding
belly in, throw out your chest and tell me I
am out of shape.

For Sam Reifler   43

While you are up on the hill embracing
blue-green acres your shadow
slips its fingers into your breath,
pinching the wick until
a smudge of smoke stands over what you held
and named after yourself.

Cold comes and presses like a cat against your ankles.
Ice socks, ice shoes,
ice where the hairs grow quietly still.

MY MOTHER DIES IN CALIFORNIA,

I GO FOR A SWIM

I stand on the edge of the pool.
All my life I've been afraid to dive in.
Now I know there is nothing
but diving and diving
headfirst into the turquoise
pool that takes my body in
to its bright maw,
where I crush myself through light,
against an edge that cries
with the shrillness of dogs
hopelessly tied.

Now I know death is what I had feared.
Now I know it is all that I have,
what I am,
and I throw myself over and over
through sunlight that slices
my outstretched arms.

COMPOSTING FOR FUN AND PROFIT

The happier you get, the worse you feel.

JOHN BERRYMAN

Delving in the dirt, it's
dangerous, the fellow said. The treasure
costs you. Buy my map and spread yourself
across the globe. Yes, leave your own
backyard and see   see   see.

I listened to him. God, I
crawled across the dry-baked ground,
hollow-brained, grasping
at concepts of shade. A spade!   A little shovel!
Oh man dig me out, I'm
breaking into my component parts.

How grit sits bitter in my jaw. Oh maw,
oh paw, decomposition of the soil is hard.
I see me sinking into
falling off the bits are part of what
is this crawling
delving dangerous, the dry
baked ground silts, it
sits within the corner of my eye sinking
making bitter grit I see this treasure sure it
costs you, mate.

OUT OF THE PICTURE

Where she has been, she drags behind her,
heavy and slurred as the speech of the deaf,
the gallery wall where she hung with
her sisters, her mothers, each
flat painted face pinned there in shadow.
She slipped from the frame that had shut them together,
shivering, follows the only track there,
that of her father, drag of his broken foot, dot
of the other, moving past
mastodons heaped in the hallways,
lit by the frozen snarl of the grizzlies,
spark of their yellow glass eyes.

And finds him, sprawled over antler bone, knees wide,
squinting at sacraments made out of mirror,
blood in his cups, insects in cases piled high
behind him, tangled collections, cut gems in coffers,
dead serpents coupling, shadow in shadow,
over his bare trembling head.
Hunting the shape of his name on her tongue,
she finds only "Father," and calls him,
stretching her hand toward his arm. His sleeve parts,
a sound like a slap or a shot. He's chanting—
stories of Greeks who split open the skulls of the most
valiant vanquished, drank down the brains.
"For courage," he cries,
lurching on thinly furred shanks. "For strength!"
She sees how the skin of his face flakes, how he is

sightless as Homer. She knows he has never
known she is there.

The sky coming in at the window reminds her the clouds'
fraying edges are her whitening hair.
Under her feet the road
beats like a heart unhinging, brings her
past slag heaps. Rivers are burning. It brings her
alongside the old silver tracks. Beginning
and ending shiver like uncoupling cars.
There is nothing
behind her, nothing
to cover the harsh
sound of the freight cars
shunted on sidings,
the crash of the freight train being
taken apart.

TARGETED

Say an arrow or something giving direction,
like that mark in the planetarium that points out stars,
slid from the ceiling perhaps just as you woke,
fixing you as its object from its place on the pale
blue wall which you'd always meant
to paint because blue makes your mouth dry,
as if you were waking inside sky-colored chalk.

And you are, in a way.
Waking in your room or the sky. Note the absence
of personal features.

The arrow sticks with you, skimming over your head as you peddle
smoothly along the path, as you wheel over
streets, creeks and beaches.
You suffer the fate of the designated everywhere.
(Aldebaran. Sirius.)
No shaking it off, though you twist and run circles,
baring your teeth like a dog.

Nighttimes, your body stretched on the bed,
you feel it slide along your flesh, along your bones,
pivotal.

You cannot see them but you know
they have made the world glass, yet it is you
who shatters.

You have not counted them, there are enough
to put their hands into the cage
that seals your heart, lift it
too high.

They stand everywhere, the pillars of a lost world
its doom,
yours.

When at last you look, the world
breaks.
Something like air burning in winter
wavers.
How would you know?

It is clear, though. They are gone
and your eyes
crystal.

GRADUATE RECORD EXAM

What have you done but peer through smeared windows
grumbling that someone should wash them?
What have you done but wait at the seashore for mail?
Now even the refrigerator steps past you, the sink
returns to the sea. The wind comes like your mother,
unbuttons your clothes.

The questions you will be asked,
you are afraid they will be hard ones.
Use your references well.
The time for studying the material is past.
It is time to get your yellow pencils out.
It is time to sit down in the new chair into which
someone has carved your initials.

First question: Whose were the voices that spoke
before you knew language? How did you answer?
Two: How has the fact that you learned to walk
holding the arms and the legs of the dead for support
affected the uses you make of sleep and of light?
Be specific.
Last: How many tongues in the emptiness? Give examples.

Put your fingers in the box when you are finished.
We will keep your face as a deposit.
The rest of you is ours already. Leave it here,
on the cloakroom hook, in the field.

SONGS SHE SINGS ARE SONGS SUNG HER

Upon the broken schoolyard lawn, kids push,
they shout, Louisie sits it out,
head green among the vines that hang from dusty boughs.
She mouths dark songs, is six, doesn't know the tricks.

Jolly   jolly   jolly   In her reader all the light-haired
        boys and girls
run sweet among straight houses. Where's this world?
Bordering these prim designs she smells another kind of story.
She is seven, this world proffered her as heaven.

Tossing her pigtails as the long swing wings her,
she stares up and asks. She asks and asks.
The answer sticks. It sits within the shadow of the leaves.
She is eight, fists clenched on the gate.

On the dock that shoots grey boards out over waters
in which all things seem to lie,
Louisie penetrates the mouths of fishes, pulls them in.
Nine years old she stands, death-dealing, bold.

The flat-planked sun whacks her. An answer flares.
She leaps to the mirror, knows that she will grow,
feels a touch, like fingers, rim her face.
Ten years sown, Louise is on her own.

Into the mirror sinks the query: I, I, I, and, asking why,
she follows, swaying underneath the vine-caught bough. Louisie,
hearing songs that gleam, that heal the broken pattern
        of the ground.

3

House on the edge of a meadow,
meadow so dry when the horses run
cuffs of dust tell where their hooves were.

House with a porch left unfinished,
road going quickly down,
taking the eye to the red iron pump
I painted last summer,
the old color rust, and flakes
of faded earth oxides.

House where the light fell
soft as beaten gold,
where I thought we'd arrived,
where we came in and rested,
soothed by the hiss of the stove,
heat sunk to our marrow.

Failed house, skull house
from which all features
are eaten away, the furniture brief
statements of loss,
parted by outbursts of ash.
Hill house, the wasps
spitting their nests into every crack
and fault.

And nothing from the tap
and nothing from the pump,
the wood too dusty to kindle,
the bed big as a desert where we
marched nightly,
across the vastness of rooms,
across the emptying years,
legs aching, our dreams
exhausted and longing for water,
approached only by motes
in the forest of light shafts that grew
from the wood of the floor to the glass
of the windows to save us,
trunks of gold up which we might climb,
day or night, over the burn of the roof
into a tender, fern-filled sky.

House encompassed by runaway plantings,
the lilac fierce by the doorway,
grass yellow with rage,
flowerbeds broken and rusted,
where I took the rough
soil in my hands and it shaped me,
where I set out bulbs like prayers
and each repaid me,
licking my fingers with its dark
or colored tongue,
leaving its love in the grooves of my wrinkling
hands become like wood
or soil itself, like loam or bark,
twiglike, efflorescent and branching.

Where as I worked
the seeds I gave up to the ground
spoke in phrases like spiral
paths the world makes
among suns, strong shouts
that flew through my hands,
arrows or angels
announcing that I
was to let myself turn as they did,
enter the intricate
chamber of furrows,
grow as they did,
upward and down,
breathe through the climbing
and sinking days,
through ages of sun.

My hands in soil,
earth made itself known to me:
House out of which
nothing could shift me,
which would forever
welcome me in.

ROUND TRIP

The iris
rising like my eyes
from quince
to lilac bush, white smoke
against the burning
spiral of the leaves,
each leaf curling
from its place of transit
to the stem & circling
the twig, the twig
the branch, as my wrist
turns upon my arm,
the earth
meandering, each particle
a turning journey, path
we take, each piece of us,
jay, flame or bark, & bearing
us in turn & turning
past ourselves & on.

I reach the stones that mark the ridgebone of the hill.
White. Red. Black. These are the colors I've been told,
but rust, rose, hint of green, all insect colors, these
are the colors that resound as I come near.

There is ankle music, beat of knee over shin.
Cricket feet, locust legs, chirp of hide, thigh on thigh.
Each year I cast one child skin behind me.
Each year I am born further away.

The trees rise dry and clear, the path lies spare.
Clenched over root hanks, my hands shine.
Porch light beneath me makes a lace of snapping twigs.

TAKING DOWN THE BARN

From over the rim of the hill land the sun
falling toward the sky makes the day.
We peel the hide from sagging sides. The wood
snaps splinters into our gloved hands.

A fear of leaves hangs overhead,
a fear of trees and hills encircling our small
home's throat, a fear of grasses living
only through their song and covering our words
in one long hasping cry of dryness.

Those who built this barn against the earth
pushed back the leaves,
they crushed the grass to whispers.
One side's off the barn now.
It lies open to the east.

FEEDING THE ANIMALS IN WINTER

Back of the windowpane, geraniums flare in the space around them,
press their leaves against the surface of the glass.
Out here it snows. The landscape lumps like flour gravy,
swells like woodsmoke white above the roof.
Beyond the gate, the field points knives against my shoes.
The barn falls back, it pulls through thinned blue air.

The horses move to meet me, slip,
the grass they cannot reach stiff green beneath the snow.
I climb the ladder to the loft, toss hay against another night of cold.
This winter's burst the ladder at the nails, the rungs will rip
and throw me to the ground; my bones know it, swaying
brittle on the wooden treads.
Chickens peck the weave of feedbags wanting corn, they
scrape their claws along the frozen ground.
My mittens, soaking, stiffen in the shape of paws.
Wind scrawls ghost ferns on the water pail.

I find my way along the fence-post rows, my chest gone white
and large with cold, the air inside me toughened, set.
The field expands, the barn
collapsing on the weather side, recedes.
My feet tight in their leather casing drop ice shapes on the stair.
Inside the house again, geraniums light fires in the snow.

THE ICE AT VARNA

Grey blocks and thin
wave-patterned sheets
fall into C-shapes
underneath my feet.
The river hurls itself in
chunks of water,
breaks around the bends.
It leaves itself like bridecake
strewn along the bank.
Flat river smell, my white-
edged footprints matt
black in the river bottom
coated snow.

Green-gold and camel-tinged,
the cottonwoods extend,
a rigid fringe, knobs dangling,
a few puffed blackbirds
thinly whistle, sound
like branch ends held across
the jostled waters.

I can't remember anything
but that I am
in this wildness. All I know is that
that is around me. All
I hear is garbled
chat: confluency, the whole
long way to sea and spring.

I stay.

I do not watch myself but river,
twitter, rippled
light, thin-branched, the sway
of this fast-cornered
water and it speaks in falling
on its curve. It greets itself.

But just this cool and skinny hand of lucent
fingertips here strokes me.
Not a language of my own. The smoothness
of the sycamore beneath my cheek is not
a touch that knows me,
my speech not this
syllabic blab of branching waters.

I can only speak these streams,
and issue words that branch and dance
the blue and perfect
ice piled overhead. Go on.
Make my own answering.

For A. R. Ammons

AND GREEN AGAIN

The wooden flowers of the yellow poplar trees
stand sharp against the flat blue metal sky,
a sketch of light like runes. High up.
What does the distance matter? Everything
is far away, your smile, the last
green hand of grass. A spell of distance.
Pine needles flare among bare branches.
I see plainly that where earth and sky touch
both are nearly windows. One can see both ways and clearly.

There, across the meadow, something stirs and is away,
already, all, away.
What's rich, what welcomes, comes to us?
The wind is all around, it circles, whistling, is itself
no presence, leaves our feet unsteady on the frozen slope.
Streams that spring here run thin as slivers,
often they sink and leave the creekbed cupped and empty.

Where are you? I have written to you years now,
said what I am able, learned how much is left
where so much is left out.
Still I dream your face, vast blue
and fully marked with light.
That is the winter dream, the summer
more your shoulders, massive, leaf-dark, green.
Come then. Always you are with me,
pulling my breath wide, gripping my shoulders.

SUMMER, NO MATTER WHAT

gold-en-seal (gōl' den-sēl') n. A woodland plant . . .

Lee and Kerry coming
past the shed along the road.
No.
It is the barn, the crib, the shed. It is
Lee and Kerry anyway
dusty in the golden seal of evening
against blue hills.
There.
It is the morning, new, true and
Lee and Kerry bearing stems of goldenseal
right past the barn, the shed, crib, shed and
all the time there is,
sealed in gold, gleaming.
Here.
The yellow dust like water leaping
barn shed barn.
No harm, Lee and Kerry,
in the morning gold, the evening
shedding light, the twilight's golden
ceiling joy.

For Karen Osborn

BEGIN ON THE PORCH

From my place at the outside edge of the yard
I hear the light exhalation of night-
sighing insects, the deep
strumming of moths against the screened door.

My forehead pressed to an orchard branch
I watch the house light through the blossoms reach
a high and rosy pitch, watch these irises
turning and turning like the air, become themselves exactly.

The world becomes itself: a landscape of language.
I stand in it reading. Black ants pass in a column, shine
like water poured over the foot of a cracked stone dial.
Here is the shadow my reed hat makes in this clear place.

And the hiss of my skirt, the faint
stir of flamingos, days
passing around me. My neck
at a slant, white and live gold.

My head at the slant orchids take toward their stalks
I walk reading. The lips of the citrus stretch
white over yellow-gold tongues, they shake
with the press of their own sweet smell.

I began on the porch. Now, the house far behind me,
woods pass, wrapped in fire. The path
flames forward. Halfway up
blood-black clusters of garnet glint underfoot.

Climbing, I think if death came like the
clouds crossing this hill, would it be bad,
I could lie on the ground rocked by failing
and gaining light, turned by the wind.

The air becomes chorusing voices, driving praise like a nail
through the lid of the sky. I believe
in these voices, in the emerging
green of the trees. Surely all will be coming.

All will be coming soon, built out of sight and sound
overlapping, of light overlaid like the braceleted
facets of cedars, like the plating on some cantankerous beast
heaving through swamps.

I let my skin unwind.
It is part of a skein thick with stars,
a tangle of spread black air that shapes itself
precisely to me.

The cat walks with me
up the back porch stairs.
I swing the door wide for us, latch it,
douse the light.

LATE SPRING TRIP

Flying past red horses by the road,
big clouds come,
the kind you can take in your hand and make something of.
Where was that rose? Patience.
It comes on its stalk, you the object.
How are we growing? Lovely. But which way?
Every object running where to else.

How we put it is:
Sky. Look. Boat. Red.
And are happy.
This is it all.
Green. Zip. Curl. Pitcher.
How is not known,
only: Bark. White. Blade. Cuddly.

My hair leaping out of my enjoyment of the air, pure lines,
my bones keeping up in their way, I'm driving
in the chesty clouds flexing as they whiz crosswise to me.
Isn't this everything? One line of Mozart
curling from the radio like fingers. Flute-fine.
Anything takes angel shape.
I feel strong.

Trees pass, on our way to meeting.
Drumbeats mouth my body. Dark for spaces, light.
This is the way to explode.
My tires licking the road, I know the highway's climbed
with me. We're sky now, honeysuckle
like dancers twining my nose.
Presence is presents. You knew that all the time.

The lines pass you, apart as your elbows,
amd when could you touch them to your mouth,
but ahead,
at the ridge of your brow where the bone becomes serious,
they hug, and how often
a doorway may poise there, a book,
upended, flutter its banner of words that are
what we see
following the lines as they pass us like chopsticks
held so that maybe if skilled
you could pick out the bits that are choicest
and gathering them like tubular rice grains
take everyone in.

TRAVELING THROUGH PICTURES OF CHINA

Let's say we start by the Grotto of the Seven Stars.
We see a lane, and over it a gate,
its four legs rising out of fields where spidery water
wheels stand over spider corn. We move
past White Cloud Mountain. Marbled towers rise.
Halls float like boats against cloud seas.

Roofs in still flame, the tiles
of lizard skin, and through this passageway
branched lattices, fair smattering of ornament, clear
oiled paper surfaces. We touch the spirit wall,
the tablets, crooked eyes that look across
to temple caverns of the Primal Spirit. Over us,

the roof pulls back in points. Bells,
lily-stiff, send waves of buzzing odor through the highest
halls: first forecourt, second, Incense Pagoda.
Here, lions like thumbs look on, and the Celestial
Queen sings in the Grotto of the Animated Rock,
in the Cave of the Morning, the Temple of Tamed

Dragon Hordes. Wave-etched,
the gods, still lively in stone dress, embrace us.
She of Great Mercy toes the ridgepole tenderly,
her eyes on Golden Summit, its descent
into a world of cloud. Road gates
sprout dragons. These bare, stretched trees

of Szechuan enfold the way to that
eight-sided Hall of Mastery whose guesthouse
waits in centuries, treasure-cool, its stillness,
waits for us among its stunted trees in jars of earth.
Behind it, hundred steps ascend the sacred
temple hill. We turn and have before us Small

Wild Goose pagoda in Shensi. Here the Monster
of Eternity guards relics, thick and dry.
Dressed stones laid everywhere against the passing
time. Graves delicate in rock. Death
making melody in stone cut
from the core of the world. And at last

the pass gate through the Great Wall.
The path again. We follow faithfully. We see
the unicorn, no milky, flower-girded horse with horn
but bronze, thick-muscled density, its gargoyle mouth,
hooked horn. The path again: Temple of Confucius,
Mount of a Thousand Buddhas, Lake of Great Light.

ROUTE 11 SOUTH TOWARDS CHRISTIANSBURG

The odor of roses at roadside folds
to your face like the thick flowered
flannel pajamas your mother
washed and dried on the line, tucked you in.

How many days like this can there be?
Even one.
Playing. Turning the wheel.
Who's steering? Me. I am.
Gas stations quiet now, places for nests.
They sleep in their graveled beds and the fields'
smile is that river,
coming along. Are you?

Two lines talking.
No end to this road, not even a smashup with you
and me tied around poles.
It goes on and on, don't we?

More and more bushes. Each
told by the shape of its organs. Reproductility.
Moving along. This is something like sliding
down stair rails in nightclothes to join the party.

Lots of dead animals, broken at roadside for crows, for us
readers and drivers, but these
opened bodies are words, dropped in the margins
where they may do good.

I like to be talked to while going,
stutter or smooth, keeping it
up now, keeping it
going along.

BENCH IN THE GARDEN

So Ida was resting and they came in.
Not one by one, they just came in.

GERTRUDE STEIN

I in the widest space seated,
like Ida, but restless, aware of the hedges
of boxwood, stretch
of the berry rows reaching through roots.

What touches, Ida? For what do we wait?

Pulling in light as a cloud pulls in water,
repeating the long
word of the berries, the rich ones, red naked
face of the day splashed on our skins,
oh Ida, I want to be idle and living
on benches in parkland,
the sweep of the landscape all language, and eat
only oysters or morsels of peaches,
lift arms up
as flying or clothing of sainthood,
staring to see
just the chair here, days static, fields soft
on our shoulders, the bushes still growing
in shapes that are as wavy as voices,
that touch our necks softly, say, "Look."
And we look.

For Richard Dillard   73

From our places we see a duck
circling the blond pubic patch of the inlet
bisected by train tracks just before Peekskill,
a world coming down, searching the frozen
ponds for an opening flash of fresh water.

Disintegration of the perfect
V-formation. This late duck
a gonner. It is winter. Even Moses
would freeze in the rushes.

Long arms toward which we fly,
dark water where we hope to rest,
as at this table, above us
something circling to land.

We glance up and wonder what draws this shade to us,
that comes in to land here, both cover and center,
in cups, in our hands, in our mouths, or in hearts
of fresh water held open, what comes here to rest.

ABOUT THE AUTHOR

Lisa Ress was born (as Anneliese Reiss) of Viennese parents in Tangier, Morocco, in 1939. Raised in a central European enclave on Chicago's North Side, she went east to junior high and high school, first in Binghamton, and then in Poughkeepsie, New York. After two years in Vienna, Ress returned to the United States, where she stapled insurance policies together, failed as a file clerk, achieved a library degree from Columbia, presided over the library of the Analytical Psychology Club of New York for three years, and compiled the bibliography volume of Collected Works of C. G. Jung for Princeton University Press. Moving from Manhattan to Floyd County, Virginia, near Roanoke, in 1976, Ress was a founding member of the Roanoke Writers' Workshop and obtained an M.A. in English from Hollins College in 1980. She received her M.F.A. in Creative Writing from Cornell in 1982, where she taught in the English Department until 1984. In that year, Ress was awarded an N. E. A. fellowship grant for poems included in this volume. She is currently teaching in the writing program at the University of California, Irvine.

Beginning with this volume, Old Dominion University sponsors publication of the winning manuscript in the annual Associated Writing Programs Award Series in Poetry, an open competition for book-length manuscripts. Established in 1974, the award carries a $1,000 honorarium, an invitation for the winning author to read at the AWP Annual Meeting, and publication of the manuscript by the University Press of Virginia under a cooperative agreement between AWP, ODU, and the Press. Virginia Commonwealth University sponsored the publication from 1974 to 1982 under a similar agreement.

Manuscripts are received by AWP and are divided among judges who are published poets. Finalists are selected and the manuscripts are submitted to a final judge who chooses the winning book. Final judges for the series have included Richard Eberhart, Elizabeth Bishop, Robert Penn Warren, Donald Justice, Maxine Kumin, William Meredith, and W. D. Snodgrass. Josephine Jacobsen chose *Flight Patterns* as the first-place selection in the 1983 AWP Award Series.

For further information and guidelines for submission write: The Associated Writing Programs, Old Dominion University, Norfolk, VA 23508.